100

THINGS TO DO IN
ORLANDO
BEFORE YOU
DIE

100

THINGS TO DO IN ORLANDO BEFORE YOU DIE

● ●

JOHN W. BROWN

REEDY PRESS

St. Louis, Missouri

To Teresa, Lauren, and Sophia,
my crew for Orlando Adventures

Reedy Press
PO Box 5131
St. Louis, MO 63139, USA
www.reedypress.com

Library of Congress Control Number: 2014932206

ISBN: 978-1-935806-59-2

Design by Jill Halpin

Printed in the United States of America
14 15 16 17 18   5 4 3 2 1

Please note that websites, phone numbers, addresses, and company names are subject to change or cancellation. We did our best to relay the most accurate information available, but due to circumstances beyond our control, please do not hold us liable for misinformation. When exploring new destinations, please do your homework before you go.

CONTENTS

• •

PREFACE

Orlando is a tourist mecca, and for good reason. More than 3 million people live in the metro area, yet more than 54 million people visit Central Florida every year to see what we have to offer. Most everyone who lives here has probably gone to theme parks at least a few dozen times by now. But if that's all you do, then you are missing out on some of the most amazing attractions you've ever seen right here in our own backyard.

For most people who live in Orlando the summer is spent inside, in the pool, or at the beach. In the cooler months you may go to a theme park now and again for a special occasion. So this book is sort of a bucket list for all the things that you should be doing here in the Orlando area before you die. From behind the scenes tours at Disney World, to monster truck rides into an orange grove, to what is known as the world's fastest zip line, to a lighthouse tour where you can see the sun go down and the moon come up at the same time. So how do you know where to start? That's what this book is for, whether you are a local or a visitor to Orlando.

I have spent many years reporting on these cool places and playing at many of the others. So I decided to put together the ultimate "must do" list while you still have time! The next time the weekend comes around and you can't figure out what to do, pull out this handy guide and start checking items off the list. I'm certain this book will take you to some of the coolest places on the planet, all within a short drive from home. Even if you've lived here your entire life, I'm sure you'll find something that will help you discover why Orlando is Vacation Capital of the World.

100

THINGS TO DO IN
ORLANDO
BEFORE YOU
DIE

Tip:
Leave the cameras in the locker.
No pictures are allowed on your behind-the-scenes tour.

TOUR THE HIDDEN WORLD
OF WALT DISNEY WORLD

If you have lived in Orlando for any length of time, you have probably "done Disney" several times by now. How about taking it up a notch and getting a "secret tour" next time? For an extra $79 on top of general admission (price at publication), you get a five-hour tour of the areas most people never go.

You get to see the "Utilidors," which are the underground tunnels that cast members use to get around the park. You will also learn about hidden messages and secret signs scattered throughout the park. You get to ride two rides during the tour while learning the secrets behind each one. When you are done, you will know things about Walt Disney and Mickey Mouse that even the most diehard Disney fans don't know.

www.disneyworld.disney.go.com/events-tours/magic-kingdom/keys-to-the-kingdom-tour/

WATCH THE SEA COWS
AT BLUE SPRING

When the days get cool, but the water stays warm, Blue Spring State Park in Volusia County becomes manatee heaven. The 73-degree spring is a designated manatee refuge for the West Indian manatees. And they come here in bunches. If it's a cool morning, you might see several hundred of the sea cows gracefully swimming through the waters in Volusia County.

You can also walk the trails and take a cruise along the St. Johns River. And if you're a scuba diver, you can take part in a cave dive in the spring, which goes down several hundred feet.

2100 W. French Ave. • Orange City 32713
www.floridastateparks.org/bluespring

St. Johns River Cruises: www.sjrivercruises.com

If you plan to visit the park during holiday or weekend hours, get there early because the park closes once it reaches capacity.

GO BACK IN TIME
ON THE DORA CANAL

The Dora Canal has been called "the most beautiful mile of water in the world," and for good reason. The canal connects Lake Dora and Lake Eustis in Lake County. It is lined with 2,000-year-old cypress trees and wildlife galore. If you take off from the docks in Mount Dora, you get a lakeside view of Mount Dora, Eustis, and the county seat of Tavares. You also get a unique perspective of the beautiful homes along the golf course on Deer Island.

Premier Boat Tours: www.doracanaltour.com
Lake County Boat Tours: www.lakecountyfl.gov/boating/guided_tours.aspx
Lakeside Inn: www.lakeside-inn.com

You also can tour the canal by kayak, but you have to be brave. The 12-foot-long gators are right at eye level!

CLIMB
ONE OF THE HIGHEST POINTS IN CENTRAL FLORIDA

The Citrus Tower in Clermont is a treasure hidden to most locals. The Orlando area first developed as an agricultural hub because of the citrus industry, and this tower lets you see how it all developed. On a clear day, you can see eight counties from the observation deck of this 226-foot tower in southern Lake County. You can even see downtown Orlando and Disney World when the skies are blue! It's a view of Florida you can only get from that high above the earth. For an added treat, head to the Citrus Tower during the Christmas holiday. The tower is lit up like a 22-story Christmas tree with a light display set to music.

141 N. Highway 27 • Clermont 34711
www.citrustower.com

PADDLEBOARDING
ALONG TURNER FLATS

Paddleboarding may look like hard work, but it's not as tough as you think. There are numerous places to paddleboard along the coast, but if you want to see some of the most pristine areas in Florida from the water, Canaveral National Seashore is your best bet. One of the best spots is north of the national park near JB's Fish Camp in New Smyrna Beach. Most days you can see manatees, dolphins, exotic birds, and thousand-year-old trees. The water is often very calm, so it will only take a few minutes to conquer the paddleboard without being hit by a rogue wave. Wear water shoes. Oyster shells can slice up your feet.

Paddleboard rentals
near the Canaveral National Seashore:

East Coast Paddle, New Smyrna Beach: www.eastcoastpaddle.com
JB's Fish Camp, New Smyrna Beach: www.jbsfishcamp.com
Paddling Paradise, Melbourne: www.paddlingparadise.com

VISIT WINE COUNTRY,
FLORIDA-STYLE

Florida has always been known for fresh fruits, and grapes aren't normally the type that comes to mind. But Lake County is home to one of the few working wineries in the entire state of Florida—Lakeridge Winery. The tour of the winery is cool enough, but you can add another notch to the fun factor during one of the festivals. You and the kids can even take part in a grape stomp right there on the rolling hills of Lake County. You get to see how the wines are made, get a sample (or two), and even get to hear a local band playing outside in the shade during the Summer Music Series.

The Wine and Chocolate Festival in mid-December is perfect for those who love, well, wine and chocolate.

19239 U.S. 27 North • Clermont 34715
Lakeridge Winery: www.lakeridgewinery.com

Other wineries, distilleries, and breweries in the Orlando area:

Keel and Curley Winery
5210 Thonotosassa Rd. • Plant City 33565
www.keelandcurleywinery.com

Orlando Brewing Company
1301 Atlanta Ave. • Orlando 32806
www.orlandobrewing.com

Mount Dora Brewing
405 S. Highland St. • Mount Dora 32757
www.mountdorabrewing.com

Palm Ridge Reserve Distillery
Umatilla
www.palmridgereserve.com

Winter Park Distilling
Winter Park
www.wpdistilling.com

Tip:

SeaWorld also offers day camp and resident camp programs, which many people are unaware of. Whether it's learning facts about marine mammals or exploring the amazing animal attractions, SeaWorld's award-winning camp programs offer behind-the-scenes, hands-on experiences with a variety of amazing animals.

SOMEWHERE, BEYOND
THE SEA(WORLD)

SeaWorld Orlando is one of the most popular theme parks in Central Florida. (Okay, you already knew that.) You can get up close and personal with animals from all over the world, including the penguins at the all new Antarctica: Empire of the Penguin and see Shamu in action. (Yes, you knew that too.) But if you haven't yet swum with the dolphins at Discovery Cove, then you're not quite a SeaWorld guru yet.

Discovery Cove is a sister park to SeaWorld Orlando and is often ranked as the No. 1 attraction in the world according to the 2013 TripAdvisor Travelers' Choice Awards! The all-inclusive park allows you to swim with the dolphins and snorkel with an array of sea creatures in the Grand Reef. And when you've had enough of the wildlife, you can slow it down with a casual float down a pristine lazy river or relax in a sunken terrace and enjoy a cold beverage. On those hot summer days in Orlando when you can't think of something cool to do, this may be one of the coolest ideas in town.

Reservations are required to get in and they only let in around 1,000 people per day, so you need to book at least two months out.

6000 Discovery Cove Way • Orlando 32821 • www.discoverycove.com

CLIMB TO THE MOON
AT PONCE INLET LIGHTHOUSE

The Ponce Inlet Lighthouse stands as a beacon at the Ponce Inlet in the small town of Ponce Inlet, just south of Wilbur-by-the-Sea. It dates back to 1887 and is still actively used as a navigational aid near the inlet's north shore. The tour of the tallest lighthouse in Florida is like a step back in time. But there is a rare event when you really need to be there—as the moon rises over the ocean and the sun sets on the horizon at the exact same time. The "Climb to the Moon" tour happens once a month and is only open to 25 people at a time, so plan early.

Don't get too fancy! Bring along your walking shoes to climb the steps of this 175-foot National Historic Landmark.

4931 S. Peninsula Dr. • Ponce Inlet 32127
www.ponceinlet.com

The only other lighthouse in Central Florida is at Cape Canaveral: www.canaverallight.org.

SEE THE SHUTTLE *ATLANTIS,*
DINGS AND ALL

The days of seeing space shuttles launch from Cape Canaveral may be gone, but it's not too late to see a shuttle up close and personal. The space shuttle *Atlantis*, the final orbiter to fly in space, now sits inside the $100 million Kennedy Space Center Visitor Complex. They didn't even clean it up! You get to see *Atlantis* and the way it was after its final trip to space, dents and all. As cool as that is, you might be blown away by the giant screens near the ceiling that show how fast the orbiter flew over the earth. A video replication of a trip around the Earth is displayed showing the seven minutes it took for the shuttles to make one complete orbit.

Make time to do the Shuttle Launch Experience while you're there. You'll know why once you do.

SR 405 • Kennedy Space Center 32899
www.kennedyspacecenter.com

LIVE LIKE A VIP
AT AN ORLANDO MAGIC GAME

Going to the Amway to see the Orlando Magic play is always a special event. But to really make it a night to remember, get the courtside seats. You get to rub elbows with celebrities and pro athletes and see the game with perfect views. You may also get picked for an "on-court timeout challenge." If you are really lucky, they may even pick you to be the "honorary captain" where you get to meet the referees and possibly even the players.

400 W. Church St. • Orlando 32801
www.180downtown.com

Tip:
If you want to take it up a level, or two levels, leave the kids at home and make a night of it at the 180 Lounge at the Amway Center (currently known as the One80 Grey Goose Lounge). Even if you're not as hip and cool as you used to be, dinner and drinks with downtown as a backdrop can certainly make you feel like a jetsetter, at least for one night.

VISIT A NEW THEME PARK
IN AN OLD LOCATION

LEGOLAND Florida is one of central Florida's newest theme parks, at a historic location. The park is located in what used to be known as Cypress Gardens, which was actually one of Florida's original theme parks. The park became famous for the daredevil water skiers and exotic backdrops like the Banyan tree planted in 1939 that now is the size of a city block. Thankfully, when LEGOLAND took over the park they kept Cypress Gardens in pristine shape. This area is how people around the world "viewed" Florida in the 1950s and 1960s, with stars like Elvis and Johnny Carson making trips to the park. Movies like *Easy to Love* and *Moon Over Miami* were at least partially filmed on location.

This is one of those attractions you may have to force your family to do. Promise them that they can watch the water ski show performed by the Lego characters but then have to spend the next hour walking through the botanical gardens with you. And when you're done, trust me, they won't hate you for it.

1 Legoland Way • Winter Haven 33884
www.florida.legoland.com

JUST DO FUN SPOT ALREADY!

You see the commercials, you drive by the parks in Orlando and Kissimmee, and it always looks like a lot of fun. Here's a news flash . . . it is fun! You will find Orlando's only wooden roller coaster, the world's second tallest skycoaster, and numerous other attractions. And yes, it's huge! Free parking, free admission, and rain checks. If it looks like a rainy Florida afternoon, your day (and your money) won't be lost.

5700 Fun Spot Way • Orlando 32819
2850 Florida Plaza Blvd. • Kissimmee 34746
www.funspotattractions.com

TAKE A LEISURELY STROLL
AT THE LEU GARDENS

There are certain times of the year when this may be the most beautiful place in all of Central Florida. It's a 50-acre garden just minutes from downtown Orlando, but it feels like a world away. One of the most interesting parts of the tour is seeing inside the former home of Harry P. Leu and his wife, Mary Jane. The tour guides are excellent and give you more insight into how Leu helped develop Orlando into the metropolitan area it is today. If you're lucky, you may even stumble upon a wedding taking place or one of the many concerts held every year on the grounds.

Take advantage of Date Night at the Garden once per month. You get to watch an outdoor movie on a blanket. Picnic baskets and alcohol are allowed. Bring the bug spray, too.

1920 N. Forest Ave. ● Orlando 32803
www.leugardens.org

SEE THE FIREWORKS
FROM A HELICOPTER

If you want a once-in-a-lifetime experience in Orlando that few people will ever get to do, then book a helicopter tour to see the fireworks. Let's face it, the Disney parks can get crowded for the nightly fireworks display. So the best spot to see the show is from several hundred feet in the sky. On some tours you get to fly over the Disney complex, along with SeaWorld and Universal Studios. But when the sun goes down you certainly want to be over Epcot to see the fireworks in all their glory. When all your friends say they saw the fireworks at Disney, you can say you saw the fireworks over Disney. The flights take off about 30 minutes before sunset, but you need to book early.

www.orlandohelitours.com

Other helicopter tours in Orlando:
Airforce Fun: www.airforcefun.com
Air Florida: www.airfloridahelicopter.com

FLY-FISHING AND GLAMPING
AT THE RITZ CARLTON

How about a world-class fly-fishing tour right here in Orlando. Shingle Creek is the northern headwaters of the Florida Everglades and the Ritz Carlton Orlando, Grande Lakes, sits right on Shingle Creek. In true Ritz style, they set you up with a fishing instructor to help you reel in some trophy fish. And if you want to make it a full "nature" vacation, you can camp right inside your room. It's called "Glamping" (Glamorous Camping), and the kids will love it. The staff sets up a tent in the Executive Suites' living room for a camping trip like you've never had before.

If you don't have any luck on the lakes, you can always try the links. The Ritz Carlton Golf Club is right next to the hotel.

4012 Central Florida Pkwy. • Orlando 32837
www.ritzcarlton.com/orlando

CYCLE THROUGH THE TREETOPS
AT FOREVER FLORIDA

"Eco" is the big buzzword these days when it comes to adventures. As a matter of fact, it's literally in the name of the Florida EcoSafaris at Forever Florida. Here, you get to pick your adventure! Choose from "The Rattlesnake," which is the very first zip line roller coaster in the United States, or a coach safari, which is a trip back in time through the conservation area (including nine ecosystems) in a giant open-air safari vehicle.

One other option is the Cypress Canopy Cycle Tour. When you see how it's done, you won't believe your eyes. It's a cycling tour where you actually pedal through the treetops. The modified reclining bicycle is attached to steel cables, much like a zip line. The good news is that you don't even have to know how to ride a bike. The canopy cycle steers itself along the cable route. This is a low-impact, low-effort way to see Florida in a new way. It takes about an hour to leisurely paddle through the Forever Florida Wildlife Conservation Area. You'll see flowers growing on the tops of trees, birds nesting below you, and a forest teaming with wildlife.

4755 N. Kenansville Rd. • St. Cloud 34773
www.floridaecosafaris.com

SURF THE WAVES
AT TYPHOON LAGOON

Central Florida's beaches are known as the shark bite capital of the world. So if you want to learn to surf without being afraid of what's lurking beneath, head down to Disney's Typhoon Lagoon. The wave pool can make some pretty intense waves, and the park allows surfing on select mornings before the masses are allowed in.

You can rent out Typhoon Lagoon for a nighttime party! It's an entire wave pool open only to you and your friends after the park closes.

1145 Buena Vista Dr. • Lake Buena Vista 32830
www.disneyworld.disney.go.com/destinations/typhoon-lagoon

Other Water Parks in Central Florida:
Wet 'n Wild: www.wetnwildorlando.com
Blizzard Beach: www.disneyworld.disney.go.com/destinations/blizzard-beach
Aquatica: www.aquaticabyseaworld.com
LEGOLAND Florida Water Park: see page 16
Daytona Lagoon: www.daytonalagoon.com

PICK STRAWBERRIES
IN LAKE COUNTY

It may sound like a lot of work, but strawberry picking in Lake County is actually a blast. There are a number of places where you can pick the fresh fruit, but one of the favorites is Oak Haven Farms near Sorrento. It's free to get in, but of course, you have to pay for your berries once you're done.

Oak Haven also has a small zip line for the kids, a play area, and a tractor ride that takes you around the old homestead. After you're done picking and playing, you can get hot dogs to roast by the fire and some of the best strawberry milkshakes you've ever tasted. And if you really want to do it right, grab a strawberry shortcake to go along with your fine dining!

The baskets they hand out hold a lot of berries! You'll likely pick more than you can eat, so be careful.

32418 Avington Rd. • Sorrento 32776
www.berriesandwines.com

Tips:

Don't rush off. Make time for the hot chocolate after the tour in the gift shop or spend a little while outside around the fire.

GET ICE!
AT GAYLORD PALMS

Florida is known for its heat. But each and every holiday season, "Ice! At Gaylord Palms" moves into town. This is a fantastic attraction that you have to see at least once, and possibly once per year if you're lucky. Yes, it may be 80 degrees in December, but somehow the crew at the Gaylord keeps this massive space at 9 degrees Fahrenheit. It's a short walk through the attraction, but you can stretch it out as long as you like (or can stand). The ice-carved characters are amazing, but wait until the end. The life-sized frozen nativity scene will likely be the crowd favorite for your group as well. So if you have friends or family from up north in town for the holidays, this should definitely be on your list of things to do one afternoon to keep them happy.

Dress warm! They provide a parka, but you will want to dig out as many warm clothes as you can find, including gloves, boots, long underwear, and a hat.

6000 W. Osceola Pkwy. • Kissimmee 34746
www.gaylordpalms.com

PADDLE THE SWAN BOATS
AT LAKE EOLA

The swan boats are such an iconic part of downtown Orlando that some people never think twice about taking them for a spin. And trust me on this one, the view from the boats in the middle of Lake Eola is unbelievable. Lake Eola is a beautiful urban water feature right in the middle of downtown, and perfect for spending a day relaxing. The brand new swan boats are very easy to paddle across the entire lake, where you can get up close and personal with some of the prized swans and other birds that call Lake Eola home. The city recently began allowing visitors to take them out when the sun goes down, which offers a great view of the nighttime skyline and the fountain show.

200 Eola Pkwy. • Orlando 32801
www.relaxgrill.com

Tips:

Plan on staying for lunch. Some locals don't realize there's a beautiful café, the Relax Grill, on the shores of Lake Eola. The café is a wonderful place to grab a bite to eat, or to just enjoy a glass of wine among the skyscrapers.

WATCH THE RED, HOT, AND BOOM FIREWORKS
AT UPTOWN ALTAMONTE

On the 3rd of July, this festival draws tens of thousands of spectators to watch the fireworks and feel the ground shake. But it's not just the fireworks that rock the crowd at Red, Hot, and Boom. The big-name musical acts that play this event would make any concert promoter jealous. Groups such as the Jonas Brothers, Christopher Wallace, Hot Chelle Rae, Cody Simpson, and many others have performed on the floating stage in Uptown Altamonte. If you plan on being there for the fireworks, make sure you stake your claim early. Parking can be tough, and finding a spot to park your chair and umbrella can also take some strategic planning.

Cranes Roost Park: 274 Cranes Roost Blvd. • Altamonte Springs 32701
www.redhotandboom.com

Other fireworks displays of note:
Fireworks at the Fountain (Downtown Orlando)
Star Spangled Sanford
Flashback 4th of July (Celebration)
Celebration of Freedom (Winter Springs)
all the theme parks

WATCH A ROCKET LAUNCH
ON THE BEACH

When rockets launch from the Kennedy Space Center you can usually see them, or least hear them, from most places in Central Florida. It's one thing to see the launch from a distance, but to get the full experience you need to get as close to Cape Canaveral as possible. It used to be difficult to get close enough to see a space shuttle launch, but since satellite rocket launches don't get as much attention, it's a lot easier to get up close.

One of the best spots to watch a rocket launch is in (or near) the water. The waters of the Intracoastal Waterway or along the beach with your toes in the sand makes for an unforgettable experience.

SR 405 • Kennedy Space Center 32899
www.kennedyspacecenter.com

Tips:

SeaWorld also has the "Quick Que Unlimited." You get front-of-the-line admission at specific rides all day long. www.seaworldparks.com

GET THE VIP TREATMENT
AT UNIVERSAL

Nothing makes you feel more like a VIP than having the Express Pass at Universal Orlando. Yes, it's an additional cost on top of your ticket price, but the enjoyment of being able to bypass the crowds all day long on any ride more than makes up for it. Universal Orlando also features different levels of express access and VIP tours, so you can choose what will work best for your family. Plus, if you stay on-site at Universal Orlando at Loews Portofino Bay Hotel, Loews Royal Pacific Resort, or Hard Rock Hotel, you receive unlimited Universal Express access at both Universal Orlando theme parks. So if you are given the choice of standing in line all day long to ride the rides or actually riding all day long, you need to get in the express lane. This is not like the Fast Pass at Disney where you have to return at a specific time. This allows you to bypass the line all day long.

6000 Universal Blvd. • Orlando 32819
www.universalorlando.com

WATCH
DISAPPEARING ISLAND APPEAR

One of the most popular beaches in all of Central Florida is a stretch of sand that is actually *not* always there. It's called Disappearing Island. And when it's there, just head to the Intracoastal Waterway on the northern edge of New Smyrna Beach, just south of Ponce Inlet to find out what the buzz is all about.

When the tide is out for the day, an island appears with soft sand where you can hang out and soak up the sun before the next high tide. On some days, hundreds of boaters flock to the island and park their boats on the shore. Some people snorkel, some barbecue, some play corn toss, and others just enjoy the sandbar that you can only reach by boat.

Be careful if you beach your boat and the tide is not fully out! You may be stuck until the tide comes back in.

On the western side of Disappearing Island, there is a canal that can protect boats from the waves.

FLOAT DOWN
THE ROCK SPRINGS RUN
AT KELLY PARK

One of the best ways to cool off in the hot summer sun is a float down the crystal clear waters at Kelly Park near Apopka. The 68-degree spring is just one part of Kelly Park, but it's the primary reason swimmers flock here. You simply jump onto a tube and wind your way down the nearly one-mile Rock Springs Run, and then do it again and again! It takes about 20 minutes to make the whole run, then a short walk back to the start. There are also plenty of beaches to hang out on if you don't feel like chasing the kids up paths. Make sure you get there early to get into the park. The park fills up early on hot summer days.

400 E. Kelly Park Rd. • Apopka 32712

Bring snorkel gear.

TAKE A PRIVATE SAFARI
AT ANIMAL KINGDOM

Animal Kingdom at Walt Disney World Resort is all about the animals. If you want a close view of the wildlife on the savanna, then you have to do the Wild Africa Trek. This is different from the Safari Tour that most people know about. Wild Africa starts off as a walking tour through the Kilimanjaro Forest with a personal guide. As the tour buses roll by beneath you, you get to walk across rope bridges to areas of the park that only the VIPs get to see. Once the walking tour is complete, you then get into a safari vehicle that takes a different path than the normal tour buses. This means you can stop and get close-up pictures of the antelopes, gazelles, and giraffes.

And just when you think the tour can't get any better, your tour bus driver takes you to a special dining area high on the savanna where you have a chef-prepared lunch overlooking the plains. It's doing Disney in a unique way. But be advised that this tour fills up early and costs plenty extra. You also get a photographer on your trip so you can relax.

551 Rainforest Rd. • Lake Buena Vista 32830
www.disneyworld.disney.go.com/destinations/animal-kingdom

SEE WINTER PARK
FROM THE WATER

Winter Park—just to the north of Orlando—is one of the most affluent cities in the United States. Many of the magnificent homes of Winter Park are hidden by heavily canopied tree-lined streets. So if you really want to see some of the most beautiful mansions in the state, you need to see them by boat. That's where the Winter Park Scenic Boat Tour comes into play. The tour takes you onto the Winter Park Chain of Lakes where you learn all about the history of Winter Park. You cruise through lush canals, see Rollins College, and of course view the opulent homes.

Make a day of it. Get to Winter Park early on a Saturday morning and browse the Winter Park Farmer's Market. Then make a short drive or walk to Lake Osceola where the boat tours begin. Follow the tour with lunch at any one of the many sidewalk cafés.

312 E. Morse Blvd. • Winter Park 32789
www.scenicboattours.com

POLKA
AT WILLOW TREE

You don't have to be in Germany to enjoy Oktoberfest! Hollerbach's Willow Tree Café lets you *schunkel* with an oompah-pah band four nights a week, right in the heart of historic downtown Sanford. Experience some *gemuetlichkeit*, which is that feeling of enjoying good food and drink among friends and family. You can order the brats, pretzels, and beer inside—or on the patio—at the restaurant rated one of the top German beer halls in the country.

If you plan to go on a weekend you need to make reservations about two weeks in advance, depending on the size of your entourage. Otherwise, you might be standing for an hour watching everyone else doing the polka.

205 E. First St. • Sanford 32771
www.willowtreecafe.com

GET DRESSED UP
FOR MICKEY'S NOT-SO-SCARY HALLOWEEN

The theme parks all have their own special events that set them apart. But when it comes to Halloween for the little, and not-so-little, trick-or-treaters, Mickey's Not-So-Scary Halloween at the Magic Kingdom is a cut above. You will see some of the most elaborate costumes on the planet. At some point in the night you will debate if you really need to see the "Boo to You" parade. The answer is "you must *not* miss it." A word of warning: you will likely be singing the song for the next few days.

You don't have to get dressed up or bring along a trick-or-treat bag (they will supply one), but a costume may make the party more enjoyable. You will leave with enough candy to keep the family sugared up for several weeks to come.

Watch the parade near Frontierland. That's where the parade begins, and it's often less crowded. Get there early too!

Walt Disney World • Lake Buena Vista 32830
www.disneyworld.com

HANG 10
AT RON JON SURF SHOP

Contrary to popular belief, Ron Jon Surf Shop didn't start in Cocoa Beach. But it certainly made the city famous. The store is recognized as the largest surf shop in the world and is a mecca for surfers from across the globe. Even if you're not a surfer, it's hard to say you've "done it all" when you haven't checked this one off the list.

While in Cocoa Beach, you will also want to drive a little further down the beach and see the Kelly Slater statue commemorating the local dude who just happens to be the most famous surfer in history.

4151 N. Atlantic Ave. • Cocoa Beach 32931
www.ronjonsurfshop.com

SEE "LADY LIBERTY"
AT BIG TREE PARK

Sadly, one of the oldest trees in the world burned to the ground in January 2012. But thankfully the second oldest tree in the park is still one of the oldest living things on the planet. The Senator tree had long been the centerpiece of Big Tree Park in Longwood but was burned to the ground due to arson. The sister tree, named Lady Liberty, is nearly as impressive. In most parks across the United States, this bald cypress would be a feature attraction, but it played second fiddle for centuries to her big sister. The tree is approximately 2,000 years old and is now the must-see tree in all of Central Florida. It's an easy walk to see the sights in the park, and thanks to renewed interest after the burning of The Senator, the park received some much-needed upgrades.

This may not be an entire day trip, so bring the bikes or walking shoes. The park also is a trailhead for the Cross Seminole Trail.

761 General Hutchinson Pkwy. • Longwood 32750

GET ARTSY
AT A WORLD-CLASS FESTIVAL

One of the biggest art festivals in the country happens in one of the nicest small towns in all of Central Florida. The Mount Dora Art Festival packs in an estimated 300,000 people each February to see the works of artists from around the globe. Many locals already take part in this event, but it's also getting national attention. The art festival has been named one of the top 100 art shows in the country by *Sunshine Artist Magazine*. The festival also showcases musicians from around Central Florida who take to the stage at beautiful Donnelly Park. Get your space at Donnelly Park early to hear the musicians! Once you have your space, walk across the street to the cupcake and ice cream shops! You may be hesitant to fight the crowds, but this is one you definitely need to check off your list.

Donnelly Park and throughout downtown Mount Dora
Mount Dora 32757 • www.mountdoracenterforthearts.org

GET SLIMED
NICKELODEON-STYLE

If your kids are always bugging you to go swimming, but you don't feel like going to the massive water parks, this may be the getaway for you. The Nickelodeon Suites Resort features a water park surrounded by hotel rooms. And yes, just like in the Nick shows, the kids get slimed several times a day. The kids are contained, so you can relax by the pools catching up on a good book and even getting a slushy adult drink right there in your easy chair. Claim your chair early because the seating area around the water park fills up quickly. At night you don't have to go anywhere else. The hotel even has a food court and plenty of fun shows to keep the kids entertained for the rest of the evening.

14500 Continental Gateway Dr. • Orlando 32821
www.nickhotel.com

BUY LOCAL
AT THE WINTER PARK
FARMERS MARKET

There is no better way to feed your family right, while helping the local economy at the same time. The Winter Park Farmers Market is truly a treat every Saturday morning. Dozens of vendors display their wares, baked goods, and fresh fruits and vegetables, while shoppers stroll along the streets around the old train depot. This is Florida living at its finest. Many people bring the dogs, grab a cup of coffee, and get their fresh produce for the week ahead. But even if you're not in the mood to buy, the atmosphere reminds you of why you live in Orlando in the first place. Start a family tradition and buy the kettle corn every weekend!

www.cityofwinterpark.org

Other farmers markets of note:

Avalon Park Farmers Market
www.avalonpark.com

Celebration's Farmers Market
www.celebrationtowncenter.com

Lake Mary Farmers Market
www.lakemaryfl.com/farmers-market

Orlando Farmers Market at Lake Eola
www.orlandofarmersmarket.com

Sand Lake Road's Farmers Market
www.drphillipsfarmersmarket.com

Waterford Farmers Market
www.waterfordlakesfarmersmarket.com

Winter Garden Farmers Market
www.wintergardenfarmersmarket.com

LIVE THE NASCAR LIFE
AT THE DAYTONA 500

You can't officially say you've "done it all" in Central Florida until you've been to the Daytona 500. It's not just about the fast cars. It's about the whole experience leading up to the Great American Race. From Hollywood stars, to professional athletes, to the biggest musical acts on the planet, they all come here for the big event. On race day, hundreds of thousands of people pile into the Daytona International Speedway to take pictures with the cars and drivers, and to take in all the festivities that come along with the race. You can even sit on the track and watch the pre-race concert on the infield. When the stadium upgrades are finished in 2016, this event will certainly go up another level.

If you really want the overall experience, then you need to get a motor home to camp out on the infield. You can also just bring a tent and camp among the thousands of race fans who spend the entire race weekend right there inside the tri-oval.

1801 W. International Speedway Blvd.
Daytona Beach 32114
www.daytonainternationalspeedway.com

Other big races to see:
Budweiser Duels
Coke Zero 400
Drive4COPD 300
Rolex 24 at Daytona

FULFILL YOUR "NEED FOR SPEED"
WITH RICHARD PETTY'S HELP

It is quite a thrill to drive a 600-horsepower NASCAR race car! The Richard Petty Driving Experience is truly hair-raising. You can drive up to 50 laps on the track at the Walt Disney World Speedway or at the Daytona International Speedway, hitting speeds upwards of 120 miles per hour as the landscape flies by in the blink of an eye. If you're not up for driving, you can do a three-lap ride-along with a professional driving instructor behind the wheel. There is even a junior ride-along for kids (ages 6-13 years old and at least 48 inches tall), giving them the opportunity to experience real-life NASCAR excitement. The experience is great fun for the entire family. Make sure to call ahead to see if you qualify for discounts.

Walt Disney World Speedway:
3450 N. World Dr. • Lake Buena Vista 32830 • 800-237-3889

Daytona International Speedway:
1801 W. International Speedway Blvd. • Daytona Beach 32114
www.drivepetty.com

COOK YOUR OWN PANCAKES
AT DELEON SPRINGS

There is nothing in the world like getting the family together, heading to a state park, and making pancakes to get your day started. DeLeon Springs is the park, and the Old Spanish Sugar Mill is the restaurant. So if you haven't done it yet, this is your official invitation to check it off your list. At the restaurant, every table has its own griddle and the servers bring you homemade pancake batter so you make them right there with your family. You can also add berries, chocolate chips, and other ingredients to customize your pancakes.

After you've stuffed your stomach, walk the park. Records show that Native Americans lived around the springs at least 6,000 years ago. In the 1800s it also became a winter resort because people up north were told that the springs were actually a fountain of youth. So there is a great history lesson you can take in when you visit the springs. Don't wait to get restaurant reservations once you are in the park. It fills up fast.

601 Ponce de Leon Blvd. • DeLeon Springs 32130
www.floridastateparks.org/deleonsprings

CELEBRATE AMERICA'S PASTIME
AT A SPRING TRAINING GAME

Baseball fans from cities up north flock to Orlando every year to catch the first glimpse of the baseball season, so it just makes sense that locals take part in this timeless ritual too. Even if you're not into baseball, this is an experience that transcends the sport. It's a day of renewal when you know summer fun is right around the corner. The look on the kids' faces when they see the green grass and catch a glimpse of their favorite players is priceless. The tickets are cheap, the level of play is fantastic, and it will certainly renew your sense of humanity. This is not just a game. This is a way of renewing your soul, even if it's just for one afternoon in the sun. Go ahead and splurge on the front-row seats. The players will likely talk to you, and the odds of getting a baseball souvenir are pretty good.

Teams currently playing in Central Florida:
Atlanta Braves: Disney Complex
Detroit Tigers: Lakeland
Houston Astros: Kissimmee
Washington Nationals: Viera

WATCH THE PGA
AT THE ARNOLD PALMER INVITATIONAL

It's the course that Arnie built, so what more do you need to know? The Arnold Palmer Invitational takes place at Bay Hill Country Club and always provides some of the best golf you can watch anywhere. The current greats like Tiger Woods and Phil Mickelson, along with legends like Arnold Palmer and Jack Nicklaus, come out each and every year to play. This tournament sets the tone of the PGA Tour season. Not to mention it's a lot of fun to be able to watch this level of golf while your friends and family up north are watching it on TV in the cold.

Don't wait for the final rounds. Go early in the week during the practice rounds for a better chance of seeing your favorite player much more closely.

9000 Bay Hill Blvd. • Orlando 32819
www.arnoldpalmerinvitational.com

WATCH A
"GRUDGE MATCH"
AT TAVISTOCK

There are a lot of professional golf events around Orlando every year, but this one is truly unique. The Tavistock Cup is a team golf event and is one of the best rivalries you will ever see. It's almost like a scene out of *West Side Story,* where the opposing "gangs" go head-to-head. Only this time, it's some of the biggest names on the PGA Tour on the most exclusive golf courses in the United States. The event is only open to a few thousand people, so the crowds are thin and you get to see these PGA stars in their true character.

Here's where it gets tricky. Tickets aren't sold to the public. You have to score these tickets from a member of the country club, a particular charity, a resident, or a sponsor of the tournament. But once you're in you get to see golf like you've never seen before.

Be there when the helicopters land! It's a surreal experience to see these PGA stars get out of the choppers and strut their way to the clubhouse.

Locations vary from year to year.
www.tavistockcup.com

BE A KNIGHT
FOR A DAY

The University of Central Florida has become the second largest university in the country in a span of 50 years. The school is big, and sports on campus are becoming a big draw, especially on football Saturdays. As the sports venues get bigger, the tailgate parties are becoming legendary. And thanks to a new conference—the American Athletic Conference—the rivalries will get bigger as well. Now that UCF and the University of South Florida are in the same conference, that game will be a "must-do" in Orlando. So pack up the cooler, load up the RV, and become a UCF Knights fan.

Bright House Networks Stadium:
E. Plaza Dr. • Orlando 32765
www.ucfknights.com

Other big games you must see in person in Central Florida:

Florida vs. Florida State

Florida Classic at the Citrus Bowl

Florida state high school football
championships

DISCOVER WHY
THE BLACK HAMMOCK IS THE PLACE OF LEGEND

The Black Hammock complex is not just a boat tour. It's not just a place to see the gators. And it's not just a place to grab some dinner and drinks. This is a true adventure right on Lake Jessup, especially when you tour the lake via airboat. Lake Jessup is where wildlife officials dump so-called "nuisance gators." At last estimate, there are over 9,500 alligators in the 10,000-acre lake. So the odds of seeing one (or many) are very good. There are plenty of gators to see back on land in the free wildlife exhibits at Black Hammock as well. You may also spot bald eagles, exotic birds, wild boars, and even bobcats on the shore as you travel through the ancient hammock. Once you're done, grab a bite to eat at the Lazy Gator. If you've always wanted to see what alligator tastes like, this is the place to find out in an environment second to none. You will want to do it all at Black Hammock. So plan on getting there in the afternoon for a boat ride, then stick around for dinner.

2356 Black Hammock Fish Camp Rd. • Oviedo 32765
www.theblackhammock.com

SEE THE STARS
ON A NIGHTTIME
PADDLEBOARDING TOUR

It's one thing to paddleboard during the day, but it's a completely different adventure at night. Imagine paddling out as the sun sets on Lake Maitland into a moonless sky where the only thing you see is the stars above. The guys from Paddleboard Orlando will take you out on their fiberglass boards into the lake towards the local stopping spot known as Dog Island. But on these tours, it's not just the stars that are glowing. These paddleboards actually have LED lights which reflect off the water and create a mood like you've never felt before.

www.paddleboardorlando.com

CHRISTMAS SHOPPING
AT THE MALL AT MILLENIA

Yes, there are thousands of places to go Christmas shopping in Central Florida. If you want to take it up a level and see the most exotic gifts on the market, visit the Mall of Millenia. The kids can see Santa and view a 60-foot Christmas tree, one of the biggest that Orlando has to offer, while you get to watch people from all over the world lug around their bags full of items. When it gets busy, go ahead and valet the car. It's worth the price to walk right in the main entrance and get the expedition started.

4200 Conroy Rd. ● Orlando 32839
www.mallatmillenia.com

DO INTERNATIONAL DRIVE
LIKE A TOURIST

Stop acting like International Drive is just for out-of-towners! It's called Orlando's Most Dynamic Destination for a reason. Some of the best restaurants and attractions in the city are lined up for you to enjoy. There are nearly 20 attractions on this stretch of highway, along with hundreds of restaurants for any taste. You can even take the I-Ride Trolley to get where you want to go, without having to fight for parking.

The official website allows you to plan your trip and gives you a map of where everything is located, so you can have your day planned before you ever get to I-Drive.

www.internationaldriveorlando.com

GET FILTHY FOR A CAUSE
AT THE MUDD VOLLEYBALL TOURNAMENT

There are numerous local charity events to take part in each year, but the March of Dimes Mudd Volleyball Tournament has become one of the must-do events of the year. Every year in August, excavators dig dozens of volleyball "pits" on a piece of property on Lee Vista Boulevard near the airport. Those pits are then filled with water where hundreds of volleyball contestants take part in an all-day tournament. So if you're thinking of getting a group of friends or coworkers together for a great time, while also helping out a great cause, this is one charity event you won't soon forget. Raise a little extra money for admittance to the VIP tent. It's air conditioned and has amazing food from local restaurants.

www.mudvb.com

ATTEND
THE WINTER PARK
CHRISTMAS BOAT PARADE

Other cities may have Christmas parades, but Winter Park does something truly remarkable. The annual Winter Park Christmas Boat Parade takes place in early December on Lake Virginia and Lake Osceola. The participants spruce up their boats in festive lights and decorations, so this is truly a sight to behold. You don't want to wait until dusk to get the party started. The festivities kick off early in the Polasek Museum & Sculpture Gardens. They have live music, food, and wine to get you into the holiday spirit. Then around 6 P.M., grab your lawn chair or blanket and watch the boat parade cruise by. If you're not able to make it onto the garden grounds, you can watch the parade from the shores along Rollins College.

www.wpboatparade.com

WALK THE BOARDWALK
ON DAYTONA BEACH

The world's most famous beach is still one of the most enjoyable places around. The boardwalk has been spruced up recently. So if it's been a few years since you've been there, you owe it to yourself to check it out again. From the new roller coaster to the Ferris wheel, the fun shops, and the bandshell, the boardwalk takes you back in time. New restaurants on the pier make this a fun beach getaway for a day. All summer long, they set off fireworks on Daytona Beach at 9:45 P.M. The boardwalk is a perfect place to see the display.

The Boardwalk and Pier:
Daytona Beach 32114
www.daytonabeachboardwalk.com

GO TO A STATE PARK
ACCESSIBLE ONLY BY BOAT

Hontoon Island is located in the St. Johns River near Deland and offers a nature experience second to none. Legend has it that Native Americans lived on this island thousands of years ago. You can still see remnants of their activities at scattered areas throughout the park. You have to take a boat to get there—I did mention that it's an island—but there is overnight camping so you can stay as long as you like.

Check out the owl totem. The original totem pole was discovered submerged in the water in 1955 and relocated to a museum, but a replica marks a burial ground that dates back 3,300 years.

2309 River Ridge Rd. • Deland 32720
www.floridastateparks.org/hontoonisland

Tip:
You may also want to check out Leesburg's Bikefest. It's not quite as big, but still tons of motorcycle fun.

FEEL THE RUMBLE
AT BIKE WEEK

Hundreds of thousands of motorcycles make the trip twice a year to Daytona Beach—the world's most famous beach. If you haven't yet been to Bike Week or Biketoberfest, you are really missing out on what makes Central Florida famous. If you ride your own motorcycle, you can cruise Main Street, Beachside, and dozens of other main drags to show off your chrome. If you don't ride, but still want to watch, get a table near one of the main thoroughfares and watch the action all day and night. And if you really want to take part, most bike shops can teach you to ride before the next great pilgrimage!

If you want to get out of the crowds for a longer excursion, the Chamber of Commerce has plenty of great rides for you to experience the Florida back roads.

www.officialbikeweek.com

www.biketoberfest.org

BECOME A CHOCOLATIER
AT PETERBROOKE CHOCOLATIER IN WINTER PARK

No, it's not Willy Wonka, but this is as close as you're going to get in Central Florida. Peterbrooke Chocolatier in Winter Park is a step back in time. A real-life chocolatier will show you how the chocolate is made, and then give you samples. You can even throw a private party at Peterbrooke for a group of friends where the whole gang learns the chocolate-making, and eating, process. You get to put on the apron, the gloves, and the hat and make your own chocolate creations. You can even bring along a bottle of wine or champagne to celebrate after the tasting is over. They also host a summer camp for kids where they learn the ins and outs of the chocolate business.

300 S. Park Ave. • Winter Park 32789
www.peterbrookewp.com

More Sweet Spots in Orlando:

Angell and Phelps—154 South Beach St. Daytona Beach 32114 www.angellandphelps.com

Chocolate Kingdom—2858 Florida Plaza Blvd. • Kissimmee 34746 www.chocolatekingdom.com

Farris and Foster's Famous Chocolate Factory—4875 New Broad St. • Orlando, 32814 • www.farrisandfosters.com

GET YOUR KICKS
AT ORLANDO CITY SOCCER

Nearly 10,000 wild and crazy fans per game can't be wrong. Orlando City Soccer is one of the only professional sports teams in Orlando, and it's growing in popularity by leaps and bounds. The team currently plays at the Citrus Bowl but will likely have their own soccer stadium near downtown soon. The team has had a great deal of success over the past few years, including winning the USL PRO league championship in 2011 and 2013. If things go as planned, the team will soon be playing in Major League Soccer. (Major League Soccer is the top North American soccer league, while USL PRO is the third division.) So if you want to get a head start and become a fan now, before they hit the big time, they certainly won't turn you away. Wear a purple shirt to the game so you look like you belong with the home fans.

Citrus Bowl: 1610 W. Church St. ● Orlando 32805
www.orlandocitysoccer.com

TAKE A TOUR
OF THE HOLY LAND
(WITHOUT THE KIDS)

Sure, the kids will love The Holy Land Experience theme park. But there is so much history to see and read about, it may be worth your time to spend an afternoon without them to get a deeper experience. The park is full of architecture that takes you back 2,000 years to the time of Christ. There are live dramas throughout the day in the state-of-the-art Church of All Nations. You can even meet the cast in the Cardo Walk at 5:30 P.M. So if you are a fan of history, especially biblical history, this theme park right along I-4 may surprise you. Take time to study the world's largest indoor model of Jerusalem. When you see how the city is laid out in grand scale, you can understand biblical stories in a better way.

Park is open Tuesday through Saturday, 10 A.M.–6 P.M.

4655 Vineland Rd. • Orlando 32811
www.holylandexperience.com

Tip:

Stick around in the lobby after the show. The men in blue start wandering around a few minutes after the performance is over to meet the audience. Be sure to take your photo with the Blue Men and their live band.

More Must-See Live Shows:

Cirque du Soleil's La Nouba—Downtown Disney: www.cirquedusoleil.com
Arabian Nights—Kissimmee: www.arabian-nights.com
Medieval Times—Kissimmee: www.medievaltimes.com/orlando
Capone's Dinner and Show—Kissimmee: www.alcapones.com

LOVE THE BLUES
AT BLUE MAN GROUP

This show is just flat-out fun. Take the kids, take the in-laws, take the outlaws, or go by yourself! It really doesn't matter. You just need to go. You are probably familiar with their act. But until you see it in person, you have no idea how talented these Blue Men are, or how hard you can laugh in one night. This is the type of show you can see more than once and enjoy it every time. Make a night of it. Plan to grab dinner at one of the many restaurants at Universal City Walk, catch the show, and then spend the evening back on City Walk.

Blue Man Theatre:
Citywalk @ Universal Orlando: 6000 Universal Blvd. ● Orlando 32819
www.blueman.com

SEE A BOWL GAME
AT THE CITRUS BOWL

Florida is known for its college football bowl games. In fact, Orlando is one of the few cities to host more than one: the Capital One Bowl and the Russell Athletic Bowl. Even if you're not an ardent fan of one of the teams, a bowl game experience is still energizing. Crazed college students, marching bands, cheerleaders, and the excitement of a big-time bowl game is something you'll never forget. Even if it's been several years since you were actually in school, you can relive those glory years and revel with the partiers at the historic Citrus Bowl. Once the Citrus Bowl has undergone its multimillion-dollar rehab, the whole experience will be that much greater. Start the party four months early by going to the Feast on the 50. It's a party in the Citrus Bowl with dinner on the soft grass of the football field.

1 Citrus Bowl Pl. ● Orlando 32805
www.floridacitrussports.com

FIND YOUR INNER PEACE
AT THE BOK TOWER

Bok Tower Gardens is a National Historic Landmark and attraction that has represented "authentic" Florida since 1929. But you can't understand how incredible this place is until you make the drive to Polk County. The tower stands in the middle of the beautiful gardens designed by world-famous landscape architect Frederick Law Olmsted Jr. It is the perfect setting to relax, meditate, or simply enjoy the natural beauty of the Sunshine State. And when the Singing Tower springs to life, it is an experience your family won't soon forget. The 205-foot-tall Bok Tower is called the Singing Tower because it houses a 60-bell carillon. They ring out every afternoon at 1 and 3 P.M. and fill the gardens with music that you have to hear to believe. If you love architecture, pay the extra money and tour the Pinewood Estate on the Bok Tower grounds.

1151 Tower Blvd. • Lake Wales 33853
www.boktowergardens.org

TAKE A DIP
IN ONE OF THE "BEST POOLS"
IN THE COUNTRY

In a city full of beautiful swimming holes, the magnificent pool at the Orlando World Center Marriott stands out from the rest. This pool has consistently been named one of the top pools in the entire country by numerous publications. We are talking about numerous water slides, including a 90-foot-long "drop" slide that you would typically find at the water parks around town. The hotel also has some of the best restaurants in Orlando, so you may want to get a babysitter at night.

8701 World Center Dr. • Orlando 32821
www.marriott.com/hotels/travel/mcowc-orlando-world-center-marriott

SEE ORLANDO
FROM A SEAPLANE

The Orlando area has hundreds of lakes and 54 million annual visitors. So it only makes sense that America's Seaplane City should be located right here in Central Florida to accommodate everyone. It's pretty common to see the seaplanes in the skies over Central Florida. Now, you can take a flight in a seaplane from downtown Tavares. The tours go about 25 nautical miles and you get to pick the route. It's not as expensive as you might think. If you want a longer ride, that could be worked out as well.

Jones Brothers Air and Sea: 150 E. Ruby St. • Tavares 32778
www.jonesairandsea.com

ZIP THE CANYONS
LIKE SUPERMAN IN OCALA

There are so many zip lines in Central Florida, it can be hard to pick one. But the zip line billed as Florida's highest, longest, and fastest should make the top of your list. The Canyon's Zip Line and Canopy Tour is a short drive north to Ocala where miners abandoned limestone quarries nearly 100 years ago. The area has been practically untouched since the work stopped in the 1930s. So this is a little bit adventure ride, history lesson, and nature tour. You'll also reach speeds of up to 50 miles per hour flying across terrain that looks like it should be anywhere but Florida. For an added thrill, zip at night when the moon is full. You can put on the glow sticks and zip through the trees and see Florida in a way that few have seen before. Better yet, zip face down, Superman style.

8045 N.W. Gainesville Rd. ● Ocala 34475
www.zipthecanyons.com/

Other great zip lines in the Orlando area:

Screamin' Gator at Gatorland—Orlando
www.gatorland.com

Treetop Trek Aerial Adventures—Melbourne
www.treetoptrek.com

Zipline Safari at Florida EcoSafaris—St. Cloud
www.floridaecosafaris.com

Zip Orlando—Kissimmee
www.ziporlando.com

ZoomAir at the Central Florida Zoo—Sanford
www.zoomair.us

ZoomAir at Tuscawilla—Daytona Beach
www.zoomair.us

DIVE BACK IN TIME
IN DEVIL'S DEN

Florida has some great offshore diving. However, one of the best dives in the entire state is in landlocked Williston. One of North America's most prehistoric places, Devil's Den is an underground spring inside a dry cave. The underground spring is always 72 degrees, so it's cool in the summer and warm in the winter. The water temperature is actually the reason why it's called Devil's Den. On cool mornings, the steam comes billowing out of the cave's chimney, looking like smoke coming from deep within the earth. Get there early to see it. The remains of many extinct animals from the Pleistocene Age (2 million to 10,000 years ago) were discovered at Devil's Den, including the bones of early man. You don't have to be a diver to enjoy the den. Snorkeling is also allowed. Devil's Den is truly a natural wonder, and it's just a short drive north from Orlando.

5390 N.E. 180th Ave. • Williston 32696
www.devilsden.com

GO SKYDIVING,
INSIDE

For people who refuse to jump out of a perfectly good airplane at 10,000 feet, iFLY Orlando Indoor Skydiving is the next best thing. It has all the thrills of a free fall without the expense of firing up the airplane. It will take you a few tries before you get it right, but once you've learned how to maneuver your body in the wind tunnel, it's quite a thrill. If you're looking for a unique place for a birthday party or get-together with friends, this is likely something no one has tried before.

6805 Visitors Circle • Orlando 32819
www.iflyworld.com

SEE THE SUNSET
ON A CATAMARAN

A three-hour cruise along the coast with a sunset catamaran tour is one of the most relaxing times you will ever have on the water. The ocean breezes and smell of salt water have a way of putting you in the "island state of mind" immediately. As the sun sets, you will likely see exotic birds, dolphins, and manatees playing in the water around you. And when you head back to the dock, the stars above and the lights from the houses are the only things you'll see. It's only a short drive from Orlando, but it feels like a world away. If you book a tour during low tide, the catamaran may also make a stop at Disappearing Island. And they even serve drinks during the expedition.

4936 S. Peninsula Dr. • Ponce Inlet 32127
www.sailingdaytona.com

GO HANG GLIDING
IN "FLAT" KISSIMMEE

You may think you need a mountain, or at least a cliff, to hang glide, but that's not true. As a matter of fact, this type of hang gliding was invented right here in Central Florida at the Wallaby Ranch near Kissimmee, where you can still take part in a tandem hang gliding flight. You simply sit back and relax in the specially designed tandem (two-seat) glider on wheels while the airplane gently lifts you into the sky. It's called aerotowing, and it's very safe. Thrill seekers come from all over the world to try it out, so take advantage of this local attraction. You can camp on the property with a swimming pool and playground on-site.

1805 Deen Still Rd. • Davenport 33897
www.wallaby.com

MONSTER TRUCK TOUR
OF ORANGE GROVES

This is one of those "only in Florida" roadside attractions that you simply have to see to believe. The Monster Truck Tour is a tour of the Showcase of Citrus in a modified school bus with gigantic tires. You pick the fruit, just like any other farm in Central Florida. The only difference is that you ride on a monster truck for a tour of the 2,500-acre ranch as well. It's not just a tour of orange groves. They also take you off-road into swampy areas, so be ready for a fun ride.

5010 U.S. Highway 27 • Clermont 34714
www.showcaseofcitrus.com

SEE THE WHITE HOUSE...
IN CLERMONT

Let's face it, a trip to Washington, D.C., can be time-consuming and expensive. So if you've always wanted to see what the Oval Office looks like, then just head to Clermont. The President's Hall of Fame is a tribute to everything that makes our government great. There are a variety of exhibits to keep the kids entertained, along with tons of historical information for adults. There's even a tiny replica of the White House so you can get a closer look at all the rooms of the Executive Mansion. Outside, take a close look at the Mount Rushmore replica. The Discovery Channel thought this attraction was worth an entire show, so it's obviously worth a trip to Lake County to explore.

123 U.S. 27 • Clermont 34711
www.thepresidentshalloffame.com

WATCH THE SCHOOL BUS RACES
IN BITHLO

Most people have seen a car race at some point. You might have even seen a truck or motorcycle race. But you haven't seen it all until you've witnessed the school bus races at the Orlando Speedway in Bithlo. And to make it even more interesting, the track is a figure 8! That means the buses have to go fast, not tip over, hopefully not crash, and be the last one standing by the checkered flag. If school buses aren't enough to fill your heart with racing joy, then make sure you pick a night when the boat and trailer races are also taking place.

19164 E. Colonial Dr. • Bithlo 32820
www.raceosw.com

GET STARSTRUCK
AT THE ORLANDO SCIENCE CENTER

It's educational, it's entertaining, and it's indoors! And when the moon is full, this is the place to see it. The Orlando Science Center is one of the top science centers in the country, and for good reason. Four floors of thought-provoking exhibits and interactive shows accompany a massive movie screen experience that's second to none. During the new Science Night Live events, adults can get into the observatory and look through the giant telescope at the stars and planets.

777 E. Princeton St. • Orlando 32803
www.osc.org

Other outdoor dining you can't miss:

Swamp House

488 W. Highbanks Rd. • DeBary 32713

www.swamphousegrill.com

Azure at the Shores Resort

2637 S. Atlantic Ave. • Daytona Beach Shores 32118

JB's Fish Camp

859 Pompano Ave. • New Smyrna Beach 32169

www.jbsfishcamp.com

Pisces Rising

239 W. Fourth Ave. • Mount Dora 32757

www.piscesrisingdining.com

DO DATE NIGHT OUTSIDE
AT HILLSTONE

Orlandoans love to dine outside when the weather is nice, and there is no finer place to spend the evening than at Hillstone Restaurant (formerly Houston's) in Winter Park. The interior is intimate, but open. The bar is generally full, but comfortable. The food is amazing and the drinks extraordinary. And a table on the patio overlooking Lake Killarney is perfect for a first date, or a 401st date. Get there an hour earlier than your reservation. Sit outside in an easy chair by the water and have a glass of wine as the sun goes down.

215 S. Orlando Ave. ● Winter Park 32789
www.hillstone.com

ROCK OUT
AT THE MONUMENT OF THE STATES

It may not sound very exciting, but a pyramid of stones from every single state is a pretty cool attraction. The Monument of the States stands in downtown Kissimmee not far from the theme parks. This monument was reportedly started back in 1942 shortly after the attack on Pearl Harbor. Governors, state officials, residents, and even President Franklin Delano Roosevelt have all sent stones or slabs from their home state. Rocks from 22 other countries have also been added. The All States Tourist Club of Kissimmee mortared all the pieces together into a strange-looking formation, which stands around 50 feet tall. The attraction was spruced up recently, thanks to a $30 million renovation at Kissimmee's Lakefront Park. Look closely for the human bones!

300 E. Monument Ave. • Kissimmee 34741

FULFILL YOUR NEED FOR BEADS
AT UNIVERSAL MARDI GRAS

Beads, beads, and more beads. Universal Studio Florida's Mardi Gras is a whole lotta New Orleans, rolled into a smaller, cleaner space! Like the Bourbon Street festival, this one runs for several weeks, so you can always fit the party into your busy schedule. During this special time each spring, Universal Studios Florida comes to life in true Mardi Gras style. The event combines unparalleled theme park entertainment with an elaborate Mardi Gras parade, dozens of colorfully costumed performers, authentic New Orleans bands, delicious Cajun cuisine, and live concerts by some of today's most popular artists. From the music to the drinks and the amazing parade, this is one party you don't want to miss. Plus, the event is included with admission to Universal Studios Florida. Line up close to the beginning of the parade. If you have a need for beads, this is usually where the bulk of them are tossed out to the crowd.

6000 Universal Blvd. • Orlando 32819
www.universalorlando.com/Events/Mardi-Gras

GET TO KNOW
DOWNTOWN ORLANDO

How did Church Street get its name? What is the Well's Built Hotel? What building downtown did Orlando's British community use as their hangout in the 1880s? If you can't answer these questions, you need to take the Downtown Orlando Historic Walking Tour. This self-guided tour will help you discover why people decided to make Orlando home. Go on a Saturday morning when it's nice and quiet. The tour is less than three miles but has a lot of history packed inside a short area.

www.cityoforlando.net/planning/cityplanning/Walk_Tour04.pdf

Other historic tours:

Orlando African-American History Tour

Orlando: www.floridaculturaltours.com

Winter Park Historical Tour
Winter Park: www.winterparkcitytours.com

Sanford Historical Downtown Walking Tour
Sanford: www.sanfordhistory.tripod.com/Links/wtour.pdf

ICE SKATE
ON THE BEACH

There's just something magical about ice skating outside in Florida. The ice is cold but the weather is warm, so you don't have to bundle up like you do in northern climates. If you truly want a unique experience, you have to ice skate on Daytona Beach. The rink is installed every fall and winter in the historic bandshell, with a view of the ocean. If it's warm enough, you can then take a dip in the Atlantic after you're done ice skating for the day. Where else in the world can you do that?

70 Boardwalk • Daytona Beach 32118
www.holidaysatdaytonabeach.com

More outdoor ice skating:
Light Up UCF—University of Central Florida campus
www.lightupucf.com

Winter in the Park—Winter Park
cityofwinterpark.org

ATTEND CHURCH
IN YOUR CAR

We have drive-in theaters and drive-through restaurants, so why not a drive-in church? In Daytona Beach Shores, the love affair with the car runs deep. And at the Daytona Beach Drive In Christian Church, you don't even have to leave the comfort of your vehicle to get your weekly blessing. You simply park your car, turn on the radio to 88.5 FM and listen as the minister gives the sermon from the second-story balcony of the Fellowship Hall. If you get there early, you can enjoy Krispy Kreme donuts.

3140 S. Atlantic Ave. • Daytona Beach Shores 32118
www.driveinchurch.net

GET SAUCED
AT THE BEST BBQ IN TOWN

The South is known for its barbecue, and there is none better than 4 Rivers. Part of the experience used to be waiting in line for an hour outside the location in Winter Park, and then sitting on the benches out back. But word got out, and this place went "hog wild." There are now several locations showcasing the best barbecue in town, without the long wait and with more seats. If you get a chance to hear John Rivers speak about how he stumbled into the restaurant business, it's worth an hour to hear his story.

Multiple Locations
www.4rsmokehouse.com

Other local BBQ greats:

Bubbalou's Bodacious Bar-B-Que
(multiple locations)
www.bubbalous.com

Caro-Bama Food Truck
(roving locations)
www.caro-bamabbq.com

Firehouse Food Truck
(roving locations)
www.firehousebbq.us

WildSide BBQ Bar and Grille
(multiple locations)
www.wildsidebbq.com

SEE A NATIONALLY BROADCAST PARADE

Only one parade in Orlando is broadcast nationwide every year. The world-famous Florida Citrus Parade is one of the biggest spectacles in the city. It's one thing to see it on TV, but it's another to marvel at the floats made of citrus fruit and hear the best high school marching bands in the country echo through downtown Orlando. This is a great way to celebrate the end of one year and the anticipation of starting anew in the City Beautiful. Go ahead and buy seats near the grandstand area at Lake Eola. That's where the parade performers put on the best show for the cameras.

www.floridacitrusparade.com

GET CORNY
IN ZELLWOOD

The Zellwood Sweet Corn Festival has taken a couple of years off. But if you still want to get your fix of Florida sweet corn in a festive fall setting, then head to Long & Scott Farms. Many people may not realize this, but Long & Scott Farms is the only sweet corn farm left in Central Florida. When fall comes around, it becomes a party! You have to test yourself with the seven-acre corn maze, enjoy the fresh food straight from the earth, and enjoy a day relaxing on the farm. The corn is also harvested in the spring, so they have great activities early in the year as well. The farm is closed on Monday, so plan ahead to make sure they're open.

26216 County Rd. 448A • Mount Dora 32757
www.longandscottfarms.com

Tip:

The leaves also come falling on Market Street during late September and early October. On Friday and Saturday nights, the street parties and Oktoberfest are not to be missed. For people who miss the magic of autumn, this is a good stand-in.

SEE THE SNOW AND LEAVES FALL
IN CELEBRATION

It has only snowed a handful of times in Central Florida. But during the month of December, the snow falls nightly in Celebration. The Now Snowing event takes place along the pristine streets of the Celebration town center. This is well worth the trip to enjoy a slice of Americana at Christmastime. Where else can you browse the storefronts in short sleeves while the snow is drifting down and the sounds of holiday music permeate the town? Of course, that's one reason it's known as Celebration. Go on New Year's Eve! There's usually a concert, fireworks, and snow . . . all in one night . . . all in one place.

www.celebrationtowncenter.com

GET YOUR GROOVE ON
AT THE CALLE ORANGE FESTIVAL

The biggest Hispanic heritage festival in Orlando continues to grow and improve every year. Even if it's not your culture, this is a festival you need to attend. The sights, sounds, smells, and experience are second to none. It's roughly 70,000 partiers packed into a ten-city-block area in downtown Orlando to dance the night away. Some of the biggest names in Latin music take to the four sound stages. Add in some of the most exotic outfits you'll ever see and you'll be livin' *la vida loca* for an entire weekend.

Downtown Orlando: www.power953.com/s/calleorange

Other must-do festivals:

Florida Music Festival
Downtown Orlando: www.floridamusicfestival.com

GreekFest
Maitland: www.orlandogreekfest.com

Dragon Boat Festival
Orlando: www.gwndragonboat.com

Orlando International Fringe Theatre Festival
Orlando: www.orlandofringe.org

Orlando Moon Festival
Orlando

Easter Surf Festival
Cocoa Beach: www.eastersurffest.com

CATCH DINNER AND A MOVIE ...
AT THE SAME TIME

Date night has never been this cool! The Enzian Theater lets you enjoy dinner and a movie (and drinks) all in one place. This Maitland theater showcases some of the best independent movies, along with other classics, in a world-class environment. You sit in comfy chairs with a table and waiter service! This place is truly one of a kind in a world full of megaplexes.

The Enzian also hosts the Florida Film Festival. So if you're in the mood for a flick that offers something different, check the list and make your plans accordingly. As with many attractions in Orlando, get there early. If you want a good table, plan on being there at least 30 minutes early.

1300 S. Orlando Ave. • Maitland 32751
www.enzian.org

BY GEORGE,
GET TO THE GEORGEFEST

Celebrating all things George Washington, the city of Eustis throws quite a party on our first president's birthday. An estimated 23,000 people from across the country show up in the small Lake County town on the last weekend of February to celebrate our country's founding father. GeorgeFest has been going on for more than 110 years and is actually the second-longest-running celebration of George Washington in the nation. Eustis celebrates in style with music and activities for all ages including a patriotic fireworks show on Friday night. Wear something patriotic, or dress up as George Washington, to really fit in with the vibe of the crowd.

www.eustischamber.org/GeorgeFest/Index.asp

STRIKE OUT
FOR SOME UPSCALE BOWLING

Bowling has come a long way since your father spent the evenings in a smoky bowling alley. Now it's about an upscale experience, and a nice dinner to boot. Kings Bowl Orlando is a great night out for the adults, complete with some of the most exotic drinks in town. You can even get fresh seafood and steaks, which is light years ahead of the hot dogs and nachos you probably ate at the alley as a kid. As a matter of fact, unlike many bowling alleys, all the food is made from scratch.

At Splitsville, you can even get sushi and margaritas while you roll a few games. This alley is in Downtown Disney, so if you need to duck away from the crowds and unwind for a couple of hours, this may be the place for you.

Kings Bowl Orlando:
8255 S. International Dr. • Orlando 32819
www.kingsbowlamerica.com

Splitsville:
1494 E. Buena Vista Dr. • Lake Buena Vista 32830
www.splitsvillelanes.com

GET FESTIVE
AT THE OSBORNE FAMILY SPECTACLE OF DANCING LIGHTS

You've probably heard the legend of the Osborne family's light show in a small Arkansas town. Some loved it, others hated it. Well, it got so big that Disney got involved. Now the 5-million-light spectacular is a must-see attraction every holiday season. The Osborne Family Spectacle of Dancing Lights brightens up the Streets of America at Disney's Hollywood Studios. Fake snow even falls as the music plays and the lights twinkle. If you need a boost to get you into the holiday spirit, you need to be standing right in the middle of the action as the lights come on at dusk. Get into the lighting area early because the streets fill up. Find a spot in the middle of the street so you can see what's going on all around you.

www.wdwinfo.com/holidays/osbornelights.htm

GREEKFEST

It's all Greek to me. And it will be Greek to you at the annual GreekFest in Maitland. You'll get a better understanding of Greek life, art, culture, music, and dance, and you'll get to eat some amazing food. You don't even have to know how to pronounce foods like koulourakia, pastitsio, dolmades, and melomakarona to fully enjoy the three-day celebration at the Holy Trinity Greek Orthodox Church. Take a tour of the church to learn more about the theology, customs, and traditions of the Orthodox faith that was established in 33 A.D.

Holy Trinity Greek Orthodox Church:
1217 Trinity Woods Lane • Maitland 32751
www.orlandogreekfest.com

LIGHT UP MOUNT DORA

On the Saturday after Thanksgiving, 2 million lights make Mount Dora shine like a star. People from all across Central Florida flock to Donnelly Park in the middle of the beautiful town to listen to music, enjoy the holiday-themed foods, and watch the lights come on with the flick of a switch. Mount Dora also has a Christmas parade the following weekend, so you can make a week of it. The lights normally come on at 6:15 P.M., which gives you plenty of time to walk through the shops beforehand, then catch dinner afterward.

Donnelly Park • Mount Dora 32757
www.mountdora.com/festivals.php

GET READY FOR CHRISTMAS
AT FORT CHRISTMAS

The Fort Christmas Cracker Christmas event is one of those nostalgic ways to get in the mood for the holiday season. And what better place to celebrate Christmas than at Fort Christmas, with the Spanish moss swaying in the breeze. The pioneer way of life is on full display during the holidays as you take a step back in time and see how Florida was in the 1800s. You'll see a replica of the fort and the old schoolhouse, while getting a history lesson of the Second Seminole War back in the 1830s and why it's called Fort Christmas.

Bring along the Christmas cards. The post office sets up a booth so you can get a "Fort Christmas" stamp on all your letters.

1300 N. Fort Christmas Rd. • Christmas 32709
www.nbbd.com/godo/FortChristmas

DO A MOONLIGHT WALKING TOUR
AT GREENWOOD CEMETERY

The people who put Orlando on the map are buried at one of the most beautiful and haunting places just south of downtown. Greenwood Cemetery is where the "who's who" of Orlando are laid to rest. And when the moon is full, the place really comes to life . . . so to speak! The city-owned cemetery offers a four-mile stroll where you can see the tombstones that made Orlando what it is today. Names like Parramore, Carr, Bumby, Robinson, Tinker, and others are buried on the peaceful grounds. The tours are led by a local historian, so you will walk away from a night among the dead with a new appreciation of the City Beautiful. The moonlight strolls are generally limited to fifty people so when you see one on the calendar, sign up quickly!

1603 Greenwood St. • Orlando 32801
www.greenwood-cemetery.net

TAKE A RIDE
ON THE WEST ORANGE TRAIL

The state of Florida is paving a bike trail that will stretch from the Gulf Coast to the Atlantic Ocean. Thankfully, Central Florida already has plenty of biking trails to explore until the cross-state trail is complete. If you want to experience the best trail rides the area has to offer, start off in Winter Garden. Begin at the Killarney Station near Lake Apopka and cross the restored railroad bridge. It's only about two miles to the rehabbed downtown Winter Garden. The bike trail goes right through the middle of Main Street, so you can see the shops and restaurants on both sides. That means you can ride a few miles, then grab some lunch. Then ride a few more miles and grab some ice cream. And if you're feeling really adventurous, you can ride the entire 22 miles up to Apopka, then turn around and do it in reverse.

www.traillink.com/trail/west-orange-trail.aspx

Other great trails:

Seminole Wekiva Trail
Park near Markham Woods Road to see the murals
painted alongside the trail.
www.traillink.com/trail/seminole-wekiva-trail.aspx

Little Econ Greenway Trail
Park along Alafaya Trail near UCF. You get a great
view of the Little Econ River, and there is even a
butterfly garden along the way.
www.traillink.com/trail/little-econ-greenway.aspx

General James Van Fleet Trail
It's a long trail with plenty of paved miles for training,
but it can be a bit lonely. It will eventually connect to
all Central Florida trails.
www.floridastateparks.org/vanfleet

SEE THE OVIEDO GHOST LIGHTS

Some say the ghostly lights don't exist. Others swear they are real, although they're hard to describe. The mysterious lights are called the Oviedo Ghost Lights, and people have been spotting them for decades. They allegedly can be seen at the County Road 419 Bridge over the Econlockhatchee River between Chuluota and Oviedo. The people who have seen them say they look like balls of lights that hover over the road. In some spottings, the lights have even reportedly chased cars before disappearing. You may not see them every time, but it's worth the night drive to see what you can find. Most spottings happen during warmer months. That may make sense if the lights are, in fact, glowing swamp gases being released by the earth.

Highway 419
East of Oviedo at the Econ River Bridge

WATCH YOUR CAR ROLL "UPHILL"
AT SPOOK HILL

This mysterious hill has become a legend around the world. Spook Hill is in Lake Wales, southwest of Kissimmee. To experience the phenomenon on this stretch of road, park, put your car in neutral, and witness how it appears to roll uphill. There is such a big legend surrounding Spook Hill that the city has put up signs to guide you there. I could explain how it happens, but that would ruin the fun of experiencing it yourself. It's a pretty good drive from Orlando. You may want to find another activity on the bucket list in that area and make it a part of a bigger trip.

www.visitcentralflorida.org/destinations/spook-hill

INVESTIGATE
NEW SMYRNA BEACH'S MYSTERY RUINS

Two sets of ruins can be found in New Smyrna Beach. The history of one is known, the other is still a mystery. The story behind the Sugar Mill Ruins is well documented. It's a former mill that dates back to the nineteenth century. All that's left today are frames of these historic structures that were destroyed during the Second Seminole War.

More ruins, with a bit more mystery, are not far away. They are known as the Turnbull Ruins. Nobody knows for sure what they were trying to build around 1776, but the foundation remains. Some think it was a fort, others think it was supposed to be a mansion overlooking the Intracoastal Waterway. Whatever it was, it's worth a few minutes of planned beach time to explore for yourself.

Sugar Mill Ruins:
1050 Old Mission Rd. • New Smyrna Beach 32168

Turnbull Ruins:
Old Fort Park at 200 S. Riverside Dr. • New Smyrna Beach 32168

STROLL
THE "COOLEST STREET IN ORLANDO"

There's a street in Orlando that is getting national recognition for its culture, history, and all around cool vibe. It's called Ivanhoe Village, alongside I-4 near downtown. It is actually centered around a small stretch of Orange Avenue just north of downtown. A treasure waiting to be found, it is also one of Orlando's Main Street neighborhoods. A day strolling and people watching near the eclectic shops and unique restaurants will show you why this stretch of road is getting national attention. If you're looking for a unique place for a Saturday stroll or a new place for date night, put Ivanhoe Village on the list.

www.ivanhoevillage.org

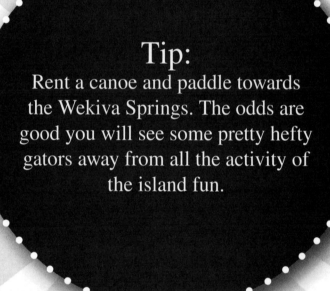

Tip:

Rent a canoe and paddle towards the Wekiva Springs. The odds are good you will see some pretty hefty gators away from all the activity of the island fun.

ESCAPE FOR A DAY
TO WEKIVA ISLAND

A lot of people who live in Central Florida swear they will never swim in the lakes and rivers (for obvious reasons). So if you have always wanted to splash around in the crystal clear spring waters, but were afraid to try, Wekiva Island in Longwood is the place for you. This island dates back decades but is under new ownership, and it's better than ever. The boardwalk runs the length of the stream on the island and is a perfect spot to lounge in the sun or jump into the 72-degree waters of the Wekiva River. They have sand volleyball courts and plenty of room for the kids to run. Plus, they have places to grab an adult beverage and listen to the music on the water's edge. This is a complete day trip, just a few miles from I-4. Rent a canopy for the day. It's a place to get away from the sun and claim a comfy chair right next to the beautiful stream.

1014 Miami Springs Rd. • Longwood 32779
www.wekivaisland.com

CHECK OUT THE CHICKENS
IN DOWNTOWN OVIEDO

This may not be something you plan a day around, but if you are in the area, why not check out the chickens. They first started appearing in downtown Oviedo in the early 1800s. Since then, the population has grown and the brood has become a part of the landscape. Heck, they even have their own Facebook page. You can often see city folk stopping by to take pictures and feed the birds. And if the kids have never actually been to a barnyard, they might be shocked to get this close to the farm. The entire city is actually classified as a bird sanctuary because of the feathered friends. Best place to see the chickens is near the Popeye's Chicken restaurant, as ironic as that might seem.

www.oviedochicken.com

GET SPOOKED
AT HALLOWEEN HORROR NIGHTS

The screams are real, but so is the fun. Where else can you have so much fun getting scared to death? Halloween Horror Nights at Universal Studios Florida is a must-do fright fest every year. The event features multiple, disturbingly real haunted houses, outrageous live shows, and streets filled with hundreds of terrifying "scare-actors." If you're thinking, "I know it's not real, so how can it be that scary?" Well, you obviously haven't been there yet! The event is consistently ranked the nation's best Halloween event in the country by *Amusement Today*, and even the editor of *Fangora Magazine* says, "I can easily say that Universal's is the best in the business." And who am I to disagree with a man who specializes in fright? Go during the week if possible. The fright fest can get pretty packed on weekends and special event days.

Universal Studios:
6000 Universal Blvd. • Orlando 32819
www.halloweenhorrornights.com

GET SPIRITUAL
IN THE PSYCHIC CAPITAL
OF THE WORLD

If you're into the supernatural and the metaphysical, you owe it to yourself to check out the town of Cassadaga. The Psychic Capital of the World is populated with certified mediums and healers. And when you walk the few streets in the metaphysical district, you can truly feel something unique. Maybe it's the calmness that brings everyone down . . . or up . . . a level.

People come from all over the world to experience the Cassadaga Spiritualist Camp to get a better understanding of spirituality. There are only fifty-five residences in the historic district with approximately thirty-five mediums living in that small area. So if you want to rub elbows with people who talk with spirits and see the world in a different light, the church services at Cassadaga Spiritualist Camp need to be on your list.

Cassadaga Spiritualist Camp Bookstore:
1112 Stevens St. • Cassadaga 32706 • www.cassadaga.org

Cassadaga Hotel:
355 Cassadaga Rd. • Cassadaga 32706 • www.cassadagahotel.net

Tip:

Stop as soon as you see the Cassadaga Spiritualist Camp Bookstore and the Cassadaga Hotel to start your excursion. There is no need to keep driving around the town, because most of the interesting places are within walking distance of these two buildings.

Other fun runs:

Disney's Marathon Weekend—Disney

Melbourne Marathon—Melbourne

Lighthouse Loop Half-Marathon—
Port Orange

Daytona Beach Half Marathon—
Daytona International Speedway

Miracle Miles 15K—Downtown Orlando

OUC Orlando Half Marathon

Dick Batchelor Run for the Children—
Universal

RUN THE WINE AND DINE
HALF MARATHON

Orlando has 5K and 10K races and walks almost every week-end. Most are in the morning through a beautiful part of town. And when you're done with the race, you go home. That's why the Wine and Dine Half Marathon needs to be on your list. The race starts at 10 P.M. at the Wide World of Sports Complex and then winds through Animal Kingdom, Hollywood Studios, and ends near the ball at Epcot. It may sound like a lot of work, but this is one of the most enjoyable times you'll ever have while exercising. Strolling or jogging through the parks in the middle of the night is amazing. After the race, you get to hang out in Epcot for a private wine and dine party. You must sign up early. Tens of thousands get to participate, but it sells out in a matter of weeks.

GO UP, UP, AND AWAY
IN A HOT AIR BALLOON

There is really no way to describe the feeling of floating on air with a bird's-eye view of Orlando and the attractions. These typical one-hour hot air balloon rides take you over our Central Florida paradise, where you can truly see it all, but hear practically no noise whatsoever. The tours start when the sun rises over the coast and before the daily storms start to brew. After some flights, you also get champagne and breakfast. Bring a jacket. It can be cool on those early morning rides in the sky!

Orlando Balloon Rides:
www.orlandoballoonrides.com

Aerostat Adventures:
www.hotairballoonorlando.com

RIDE THE WAVES
IN KISSIMMEE

Who says you need a beach to surf? And who says you need to be outside? The FlowRider Wave Simulator at Fantasy Surf in Kissimmee lets you get up on the board without having to worry about the weather or the wave heights. The cool kids call it "flowriding," and it's surfing, wakeboarding, snowboarding, and skateboarding all rolled into one! You don't even have to know how to surf, because they can teach you on location. But if you already know what you're doing, the waves are enough to give you a thrill. Better yet—no sharks.

5151 Kyngs Heath Rd. • Kissimmee 34746
www.ultimateindoorwave.com

RIDE THE GLASS BOTTOM BOAT
AT SILVER SPRINGS

The springs aren't as beautiful as they used to be, but that's a little misleading. Silver Springs is still one of the most beautiful places on the planet and has to be seen to be truly understood. There are seven major springs here that pump out 550 million gallons of water per day. The best way to see "Florida's oldest attraction" is on board the world-famous glass bottom boats. This attraction near Ocala has been drawing crowds since the 1800s and was even the beautiful backdrop to movies like *Creature from the Black Lagoon* and *Tarzan*. The waters are still billed as 99.8 percent pure, so it's as close to perfection as you can get. The park is being added to the network of Florida's state parks, so Silver Springs is receiving millions in renovations and upgrades.

5656 E. Silver Springs Blvd. • Silver Springs 34488
www.silversprings.com

Tip:
Watch old videos of the *Sea Hunt* TV show to build the anticipation. Many parts of the series were shot on location at Silver Springs.

Other gator-themed attractions:

Reptile Discovery Center
2710 Big John Dr. • DeLand 32720
386-740-9143 • www.reptilediscoverycenter.com

Jungle Adventures Animal Park
26205 E. Colonial Dr. • Christmas 32709
407-568-2885 • www.jungleadventures.com

WRESTLE A GATOR
...SORT OF

Gatorland is one of the original Florida attractions, and it's awesome. There are hundreds of gators spread out all across the alligator-themed park. You can get up close and personal, sitting on the back of a gator. You even get to hold its snout for pictures. The park has plenty of attractions that will entertain people of all ages, but one of the highlights is certainly the Gator Wrestlin' Experience. You will also see exotic birds, Florida panthers, and some of the biggest snakes on the planet. They even have a zip line tour that whizzes you right over the heads of the giant reptiles. Get to the wrestlin' show early to get your picture on the back of a gator. It's as safe as it can get, and the kids will show the picture to everyone they know.

14501 S. Orange Blossom Trail ● Orlando 32837 ● 800-393-5297
www.gatorland.com

Other gator-themed attractions:
Reptile Discovery Center:
2710 Big John Dr. ● DeLand 32720 ● 386-740-9143
www.reptilediscoverycenter.com

Jungle Adventures Animal Park:
26205 E. Colonial Dr. ● Christmas 32709 ● 407-568-2885
www.jungleadventures.com

SUGGESTED ITINERARIES

HIT THE BEACH

OUTDOOR EXPEDITIONS

● ●

DATE NIGHT

Leu Gardens, 18

Hillstone, 83

Ice Skating on the Beach, 88

Upscale Bowling, 100

Hot Air Balloon Rides, 120

Walk in the Snow in Celebration, 95

Enzian Theater, 98

ACTIVITIES
BY REGION

ORLANDO (CENTRAL)

NORTH

• •

SOUTH

BEACHES

• •

ACTIVITIES
BY SEASON

Despite Orlando's sunny year-round weather, there are still activities reserved for specific times of the year. Here are a few of these seasonal events:

WINTER

Manatees at Blue Spring State Park, 4

Mount Dora Art Festival, 40

Bowl Games at Citrus Bowl, 68

Outdoor Ice Skating, 88

Citrus Bowl Parade, 92

Christmas Activities, 6, 54, 57, 95, 103, 104

SPRING

Daytona 500, 44

Spring Training Baseball, 47

Arnold Palmer Invitational, 48

Tavistock Cup Golf Match, 49

• •

SUMMER

Disappearing Island, 32

Wekiva Island, 113

Fly-fishing at the Ritz, 20

Paddleboarding Along the Coast, 7, 53

Surf at Typhoon Lagoon, 22

Everything else unless it's too hot!!

FALL

Halloween Horror Nights, 115

UCF Knights Football, 50

Light Up Mount Dora, 103

Zellwood Sweet Corn Festival, 93

Ice! at Gaylord Palms, 25

Mickey's Not-So-Scary Halloween, 37

● ●

INDEX

● ●

• •